Edited by Jane Griffiths

Traditional Fiddle

A practical introduction to styles from England, Ireland, Scotland, and Wales

MUSIC DEPARTMENT

OXFORD
UNIVERSITY PRESS

OXFORD
UNIVERSITY PRESS

Great Clarendon Street, Oxford OX2 6DP,
United Kingdom

Oxford University Press is a department of the University of Oxford.
It furthers the University's objective of excellence in research, scholarship,
and education by publishing worldwide. Oxford is a registered trade mark of
Oxford University Press in the UK and in certain other countries

This collection © Oxford University Press 2015

Jane Griffiths has asserted her right under the
Copyright, Designs and Patents Act, 1988, to be identified as the Editor of this Work
Each author has asserted his/her right under the Copyright, Designs and
Patents Act, 1988, to be identified as the Author of their Work(s)

Database right Oxford University Press (maker)

First published 2015

Impression: 1

All rights reserved. No part of this publication may be reproduced,
stored in a retrieval system, or transmitted, in any form or by any means,
without the prior permission in writing of Oxford University Press

Permission to perform this work in public (except in the course of divine worship) should normally be
obtained from the Performing Right Society Ltd (PRS) at www.prsformusic.com or
a local performing right licensing organization, unless the owner or the occupier
of the premises being used already holds a licence from such an organization.
Likewise, permission to make and exploit a recording must be obtained in advance from the
Mechanical-Copyright Protection Society Ltd (MCPS) at www.prsformusic.com or
a local mechanical copyright licensing organization

Enquiries concerning reproduction outside the scope of the above
should be directed to the Music Rights Department, Oxford University Press, at
music.permissions.uk@oup.com or at the address above

ISBN 978-0-19-339279-3

Music and text origination by Julia Bovee

Printed in Great Britain on acid-free paper by
Halstan & Co. Ltd, Amersham, Bucks.

CD credits

All tracks recorded by the artist unless specified otherwise.

Tracks 1–4:	Nancy Kerr, recorded by Tom A. Wright at Powered Flight Music (www.poweredflightmusic.com)
Tracks 5–7:	Jenna Reid, recorded by Angus John Lyon
Tracks 8–13:	John Dipper
Tracks 14–23:	Liz Doherty
Tracks 24–8:	Aidan O'Rourke
Tracks 29–32:	Siân Phillips, recorded by Colin Fletcher at Starling Audio (www.starlingaudio.com)
Tracks 33–8:	Patsy Reid
Tracks 39–43:	Kevin Burke, recorded by John Brennan at East Woods Recording, Pound Ridge, NY

Companion Website backing tracks: Jon Fletcher (guitar), recorded by Colin Fletcher at Starling Audio.

All tracks edited, mixed, and mastered by Colin Fletcher at Starling Audio using Ardour (www.ardour.org).

Preface

I first heard an Irish fiddler in a pub when I was seven years old and away on holiday, and I was fascinated by the player's vitality and inventiveness. Having already started classical violin lessons, I pestered my parents for a book of traditional tunes as soon as we returned home. Over the following months, I learned many of the tunes, playing them exactly as written, frantically bowing them out—and wondered why they failed to come to life. My classical studies then took over, and it was not until a decade later, as a student, that I came back to traditional music. Through listening to many wonderful players in pub sessions, I began to realize why my experience with that first book of tunes had been so frustrating: it had given me the skeleton of each melody, but no inkling of the way a traditional player bows, ornaments, and varies those bare bones to breathe life into the tune.

In an attempt to understand the fiddler's approach, I began a haphazard adventure, transcribing tunes, attending workshops, and asking endless questions. How I wished for a book that explained the basics! Unsurprisingly, all these years later, I seized upon the opportunity to compile and edit this volume, which gives fledgling fiddlers expert guidance as they make their first forays into traditional playing styles from England, Ireland, Scotland, and Wales. The eight contributors to this book are all world-renowned fiddlers; the advice they give in these pages, coupled with their beautiful playing on the CD, provides step-by-step practical help and immense inspiration for the novice fiddler.

Acknowledgements

First and foremost, enormous thanks to Kevin Burke, John Dipper, Liz Doherty, Nancy Kerr, Aidan O'Rourke, Siân Phillips, Jenna Reid, and Patsy Reid for so generously sharing your expertise in this book. It has been a delight and a privilege to work with you all, and thank you for enduring my endless editorial interventions with such stoical good humour.

I owe much gratitude to David Blackwell, former Head of the Music Department at OUP, for inviting me to compile and edit this volume. Thank you also to my editors at OUP—Laura Jones, Philip Croydon, and Chris Corcoran—for their invaluable help and patience, and thank you to all at OUP who have been involved in the production of this book; I absolutely appreciate the team effort. Thank you also to Starling Audio for your technical and musical wizardry regarding the CD.

Thank you to all the dear friends and musical comrades who have nurtured, shared, and sustained my love for traditional music: Andy Letcher, Abbie Lathe, Lisa Fitzgibbon, Sharron Kraus, Doug Lang, Jon Fletcher, Jim Penny, Jo Hamilton, Barney Morse-Brown, Charlie Henry, Roger Claridge, and Rosanna Caltabiano. Additional gratitude is due to Jon Fletcher for the guitar chords and your beautiful playing. Finally, a heartfelt thank you to Colin Fletcher, for just about everything.

JANE GRIFFITHS

The contributors

Kevin Burke

Kevin Burke has been at the forefront of traditional Irish music for 40 years. During his long career, he has earned international acclaim as a solo performer, teacher, and as a member of some of traditional music's most admired and respected groups, including the Bothy Band, Patrick Street, and Celtic Fiddle Festival, with whom he has made several influential recordings. He has also worked with Grammy-award winner Tim O'Brien in The Crossing. In 2007, Kevin set up his own record label, Loftus Music; its first album, *Across the Black River*, was hailed by the *New York Times* as one of the top world music releases of 2007. Kevin's contribution to traditional music was acknowledged in 2002 by The National Endowment for the Arts, when he was awarded a National Heritage Fellowship, the USA's highest honour for excellence in folk and traditional arts.

John Dipper

A respected performer, composer, and teacher, John grew up steeped in the musical traditions of southern England. His unique style and compositions convey a deep understanding of, and passion for, indigenous English music. A founder member of the English Acoustic Collective, John performs with award-winning instrumentalist Luke Daniels; with acclaimed singer–guitarist James Patterson; and with renowned storytellers Hugh Lupton and Nick Hennessey. He is a member of the ground-breaking string quartet Methera, which performs traditional music from England and beyond, and he is a featured artist on several film scores, including *The Hobbit*. John has collaborated with numerous artists, among them Chris Wood, Karen Tweed, Nic Jones, and Martyn Wyndham-Read. He is a much sought-after tutor and has taught at the Australian National Folk Festival, Sidmouth International Festival, and Ashokan. He regularly teaches on the Folk and Traditional Music degree course at Newcastle University and for the World and Irish music MA at Limerick University.

Liz Doherty

Dr Liz Doherty is a distinguished fiddle player and teacher. She was taught by Donegal master Dinny McLaughlin and is known for her distinctive style. Liz has played and recorded with renowned Irish bands Nomos, The Bumblebees, and Fiddlesticks, and has released two solo albums. She has also performed for Riverdance and with international ensemble String Sisters. An in-demand tutor, she has taught at many international events, among them the Valley of the Moon fiddle camp, the Australian National Folk Festival, Celtic Colours, Celtic Connections, and Willie Clancy Week. Liz has lectured on traditional music internationally and is currently Lecturer in Traditional Music at the University of Ulster in Derry. She has worked as a consultant for numerous traditional music projects in Ireland, including as Director of the 2012 North Atlantic Fiddle Convention in Donegal. Liz is also author of the encyclopedia *The Cape Breton Fiddle Companion*, and is currently leading research on performance-related injuries for the Safe Trad project.

Nancy Kerr

Influential fiddler–singer Nancy Kerr was born in London but spent formative years in Northumberland, where she developed a love of the tunes and songs from that region. Nancy became well known for her duo with Eliza Carthy when the pair were teenagers. She is a multiple BBC Folk Award winner, including 'Best Duo' in 2003 and 2011 with bouzouki player James Fagan, and 'Best Group' and 'Best Album' with folk supergroup The Full English in 2014. She now collaborates with Martin Simpson, Andy Cutting, and the English Folk Dance and Song Society project The Elizabethan Session. Her version of eighteenth-century lullaby *Dance to your Daddy* was Gareth Malone's 'inheritance track' on BBC Radio 4.

Aidan O'Rourke

Aidan O'Rourke, loved for his warm, lyrical fiddle style, stands at the centre of the modern Scottish folk music revival. Uniting Aidan's musical activity is his deep fascination with Scottish culture and landscape. By the age of 14, having already won multiple prizes on the Scottish competition circuit, he was touring the UK, Europe, and America. Aidan is best known for his work with the ground-breaking trio Lau, which has won 'Best Group' in the BBC Radio 2 Folk Awards a record-breaking four times. Aidan is also a highly regarded composer; named 'Composer of the Year' at the 2011 Scots Trad Music Awards, he has been commissioned by many prestigious organizations, among them Celtic Connections and the Sage Gateshead. Aidan is an experienced teacher; he co-founded the fiddle camp Blazin' in Beauly and has tutored at Celtic Connections and Cambridge Folk Festival. Aidan was named 'Musician of the Year' at the 2014 BBC Radio 2 Folk Awards.

Siân Phillips

Siân's extensive experience of Eisteddfodau, barn dances (twmpathau), and folk dance accompaniment has given her an unrivalled knowledge and understanding of Welsh traditional music and its interpretation (although her earliest musical influences were Pink Floyd and Stéphane Grappelli!). She has performed as a solo artist and with various bands at festivals and concerts throughout the UK, Europe, and America, and has taught at numerous workshops and seminars, including Fiddles on Fire and Fiddles at Witney. In addition, she has featured in several BBC Cymru television and BBC Wales radio folk programmes. Siân currently works as an in-demand session musician and teacher based in north Oxfordshire.

Jenna Reid

Shetland fiddler Jenna Reid is one of the brightest young talents to grace the traditional music scene. Since winning 'Best Up and Coming Artist' at the Scots Trad Music Awards in 2005, she has released three solo albums and has subsequently been nominated for 'Best Instrumentalist'. A protégée of the greatest names in Shetland fiddling, Jenna has appeared all over the world with the award-winning band Blazin' Fiddles and chamber folk quartet RANT. She has also performed alongside Aly Bain on the renowned TV series *Transatlantic Sessions*. Jenna is an experienced teacher, running a summer school in Shetland. Alongside her sister Bethany, she has also curated the Shetland Fiddle Frenzy festival.

Patsy Reid

Hailing from Perthshire, Patsy Reid specializes in performing, writing, and teaching traditional Scottish music. She is the youngest-ever winner of the prestigious Glenfiddich Fiddle Championship and a founding member of Scottish band Breabach. She has collaborated with the best of the UK folk scene, performing at many festivals, including the 2012 London Olympic Festival and the 2014 Commonwealth Games closing ceremony, as well as annual appearances at Celtic Connections. Her third solo album, *The Brightest Path*, was nominated for 'Album of the Year' at the 2014 Scots Trad Music Awards and included in *Songlines* magazine's list of '10 essential Scottish albums'. Patsy's qualifications include a PGCE with Specialist String Teaching and a post-graduate diploma in classical violin performance from the Royal Northern College of Music. Despite a busy performance schedule, she makes time to teach musicians of all ages, contributing to Newcastle University's Folk and Traditional Music degree, the University of the Highlands and Islands Applied Music degree, and Alasdair Fraser's Fiddle and Cello Week, as well as teaching privately at home in Perth.

Jane Griffiths (Editor and compiler)

Jane Griffiths studied violin and piano at Chetham's School of Music before becoming interested in traditional fiddle. Her unique style has led her to perform nationally and further afield with musicians from many genres, among them Andy Letcher, Sharron Kraus, Abbie Lathe, Jon Fletcher, and Lisa Fitzgibbon. She works regularly as a session musician and has recorded for, among others, Maddy Prior, Simon Emmerson, Duotone, Amy Macdonald, and Stornoway. She currently plays with dark English folk band Telling The Bees, and with Wod, a trio for French and Breton dance. Jane is also a highly experienced violin, fiddle, and piano teacher, and freelance music editor.

Contents

How to use this book and CD	viii
Playing traditional fiddle	ix
The tunes	x
Learning by ear	xi
Some final thoughts	xii

1. Nancy Kerr: Northumbrian 3/2 hornpipes — 1
- Rusty Gulley (workshop) — 2
- Lang Stayed Away — 3
- Bob and Joan — 3

2. Jenna Reid: Shetland reels — 4
- Aa the Ships ir Sailin' (workshop) — 5
- Shelder Geö — 6
- Mak a Kishie Needle, Dye — 6

3. John Dipper: Southern English Playford and morris dance tunes — 7
- Argiers (workshop) — 8
- Old Tom of Oxford — 10
- Mount Hills — 10

4. Liz Doherty: Donegal reels — 11
- Leslie's Reel (workshop) — 12
- Dinkie Dorrian's — 14
- The Boys of Malin — 15

5. Liz Doherty: Donegal jigs — 17
- Johnny Boyle's Jig (workshop) — 18
- Con Cassidy's Jig — 20
- The Black Rogue — 21

6. Aidan O'Rourke: West Highland strathspeys and a reel — 23
- Mrs MacLeod's Strathspey (workshop) — 24
- Niel Gow's Wife — 26
- Lochiel's Awa' Tae France — 27

7. Siân Phillips: Welsh hornpipes — 29
- Gower Reel (workshop) — 30
- Swansea Hornpipe — 31
- Pibddawns y Car Gwyllt — 32

8. Patsy Reid: North-East Scottish slow airs — 33
- The Marchioness of Huntly's Favourite (workshop) — 34
- Bovaglie's Plaid — 36
- The Weeping Birches of Kilmorack — 37

9. Kevin Burke: Sligo reels — 39
- Boys of the Lough (workshop) — 40
- Pigeon on the Gate — 42
- Sligo Maid — 43

How to use this book and CD

Each chapter begins with a brief overview of the relevant fiddle style and information on the three tunes in the chapter. The first tune is presented in a 'workshop' format, with key stylistic features, including ornaments and bowing, discussed and illustrated. The subsequent tunes draw upon the same features. At the end of each workshop there is a 'Next steps' section designed to encourage further awareness of stylistic features (see notes on the CD, below).

The three tunes work as individual pieces or strung together into what traditional players call a 'set'. For single tune playing, 'End' bars are given when the tune does not resolve onto the tonic. Instructions are also supplied for putting the tunes together. See also 'Sets of tunes' on p. xi.

The chapters are arranged in a progressive order of difficulty. In addition, the concluding chapter (Sligo reels) not only features bowing and ornamentation introduced in the Sligo workshop, but also draws upon elements explored in earlier chapters. There is a degree of natural flexibility built into the tunes; it is possible to omit some of the more demanding ornamentation, if necessary, while still engaging with the broader stylistic elements.

The CD provides accompanied recordings of the three tunes in each chapter. Each tune is played through twice: the first time as given in the book, the second time with varied ornamentation and bowing. This reflects a traditional fiddler's approach and gives ideas on how to extend the workshop material, as highlighted in the 'Next steps' section at the end of each workshop, which helps you identify different features in the second playing. The CD also includes demonstration recordings of the ornaments and bowing patterns that may be unfamiliar to classical players. Track numbers for the performances and demonstrations are given in each chapter. Guitar backing tracks for all of the tunes, with the exception of the slow airs in Chapter 8, are available to download from the Companion Website: www.oup.co.uk/companion/traditionalfiddle. As these slow airs make extensive use of rubato, it is not appropriate to supply backing tracks as they would prevent exploration of this key stylistic feature. Practice tracks recorded at a slower tempo are also available on the Companion Website for the tunes in Chapter 9.

For those who wish to explore further, the Companion Website also includes lists of the contributors' recordings, other related listening, and reading suggestions for each chapter, alongside further information on each contributor.

Playing traditional fiddle

The music

Unlike in classical music, where you learn to play exactly what is written on the page, traditional musicians regard the tune (notated or learned by ear) as only part of the story. It is an intrinsic part of traditional music to add ornamentation to the tune, to repeat it, and to introduce rhythmic and melodic variation as you do so. For experienced players, this process—although shaped by stylistic knowledge and convention—is largely spontaneous.

For these reasons, tune books conventionally give only the 'skeleton' of the piece, i.e. the notes, with no articulation, ornamentation, or any other detail. However, as this is a book for teaching and learning, only 'realized' versions of the tune are provided, with bowing and ornamentation added. Both left-hand and bowed ornaments are denoted by symbols above the stave wherever possible and, because fiddlers from different regions sometimes call the same ornament by different names (and vice versa!), they are cross-referenced between chapters where appropriate. The contributors explain carefully why and how such embellishments are used, so that you learn how to transfer the techniques and ideas when encountering a tune in skeleton form.

Using ornamentation

Once you've learned how to execute a particular embellishment, you choose where to put it and how often to play it; indeed, this is one of the simplest ways to start developing your ability to vary the tune. However, you do need to think about why you are using a particular ornament and what effect you intend to produce, e.g. is it to add interest to a repeating phrase, or to accentuate a particular rhythm? Listening to the CD and the recordings listed on the website is crucial in helping you learn how to do this stylistically.

It's all in the bow

For fiddlers, the creative essence at the heart of traditional music means that the bowing is not devised in advance, but as the tune progresses, and that when playing together, fiddlers rarely use the same bowing as each other. This in no way implies that the articulation is unimportant; it's often said that fiddle playing is all about the right hand, and most fiddlers would agree that it's what the player does with the bow that gives traditional playing its particular character. While each fiddler's bowing is unique, there are certain patterns common to players from the same region that provide the backbone of any distinctly recognizable regional style, and the workshops in this book introduce some of the basic ways in which the bow is used to bring life to traditional tunes in a regional context.

On the subject of bowing, it is common to see traditional fiddlers holding their bow further away from the frog than classical players; a 'high' hold shifts the balance of the stick, and some fiddlers find this more comfortable for playing faster tunes in the middle and top half of the bow. However, there are no hard and fast rules, as evidenced by the bow-holds of the contributors to this book. For example, Nancy Kerr holds her bow several inches above the frog, while John Dipper holds his like a classical player. In short, there is no need to adjust the bow-hold to play this music, but it is worth experimenting to see how the balance changes, how this affects the way the bow works, and whether this helps you create the desired bowing effects.

Open strings

Unlike in classical violin playing, where open strings are generally avoided, traditional players embrace them, enjoying the ringing sound and the additional string-crossings as a conscious part of their overall approach. Few of the players who contribute to this book use 4th fingers in place of open strings except on one or two occasions, as marked. If no 4th-finger indication is given, then play the relevant open string.

Intonation

Traditional musicians often play with untempered intonation; the third and seventh notes of the scale are often noticeably different from how they would sound in 12-tone equal temperament, and this contributes much to the character of traditional music. Most of the fiddlers in this book use untempered scales, as you will hear on the CD. This is not something you need to replicate when starting out—but it is important that you don't think of it as being simply 'out of tune' playing!

Vibrato

As with holding the bow, vibrato varies between individual fiddlers. Generally, very few Irish players use vibrato as a matter of course, although some will introduce it on slower tunes. It seems that vibrato is used more in Scottish styles, particularly those with a historical link to classical playing, e.g. North-East style. Of the contributors to this book, Kevin Burke uses vibrato occasionally, and Nancy Kerr uses it in a particularly individual and distinctive fashion, often as an emphasis after the start of the note. However, you should err on the side of caution and limit its use; enjoy the clean, pure sound of the instrument.

Dynamics

The tunes in this book (with the exception of slow airs) would originally have been used for dancing, and therefore the primary aim, particularly in the days before amplification, would have been to play them loudly enough to be heard above the stamping of the dancers' feet. Dynamics are therefore not an integral part of traditional playing in the way that they are in classical performance. However, traditional players do use dynamics; it again rather depends on the individual player, and the setting. Certainly, many of the contributors to this book make instinctive and varied use of dynamics when performing. However, you do not need to consider this when starting out.

The tunes

Tune types

There are a number of different tune types covered by this book. They are:

hornpipes, which are in 4/4 but have a 2/2 feel (and are sometimes notated in 2/2)
3/2 hornpipes
jigs (also known properly as double jigs), which are in 6/8
morris tunes in 2/2
Playford tunes in 2/2
reels, which are written in 4/4 time in this book but have a 2/2 feel (and are sometimes notated in 2/2)
slow airs, in a variety of time signatures
strathspeys, which are in 4/4.

The dance origins of these tunes still determine, to some extent, the speeds at which they are played. There is a misconception that traditional tunes are always played at great speed; this is not so, and dancers will never thank you for playing too fast! In reality, a range of speeds is acceptable, governed by the occasion and the individual player. On the CD, the contributors perform their tunes at the slower end of that range. The best way to get a feel for the usual speeds is to listen to the recordings listed on the Companion Website.

Structure

Traditional tunes are often structured straightforwardly, with just two sections, although there can be more. These are described as 'the A part', 'the B part', etc., as labelled here. Each section, which is usually repeated, tends to be 4, 8, or 16 bars/measures. Tunes are normally played through more than once, and often several times, with the repeats observed on each playing. It is convention in pub 'sessions' (informal gatherings of musicians) that tunes are led by one or two players and are played through three times; at the end of the third time, everyone else stops briefly to listen to the leaders and find out which tune is coming next in the set (see below), when they'll join in playing again. There are no hard and fast rules on how to end tunes played either individually or as a set; they do usually resolve onto the home note, but how you get there is up to the individual—you can slow them down or keep in strict tempo right to the end.

Sets of tunes

As discussed above, the tunes in this book can be played as individual pieces or (with the exception of the slow airs) as a 'set', i.e. strung together, one tune after the other, moving seamlessly from one to the next. It is usual for traditional musicians to play tunes in this way due to the dance origins of most traditional music; changing tune part-way through the dance can give the dancers a burst of energy.

The general rule when putting together a set is that the same types of tune should be used, e.g. you might play a set of reels, or a set of jigs, but not chop and change between the two types. Having said that, different tune types with the same time signature are put together. It's common to put strathspeys and reels together, for example, as Aidan O'Rourke suggests in his chapter on West Highland fiddling.

Another factor to consider is how the keys work. It's often a good idea to have some modulation between tunes to create a sense of journey and momentum. Kevin Burke's tunes are a good example of this: 'Boys of the Lough' is in D major, then the set moves to E Dorian ('Pigeon on the Gate'), and then to A Dorian ('Sligo Maid'). The best way to hear how tunes are played together in a set is to listen to the recordings listed on the Companion Website.

Learning by ear

Learning by ear is a fundamental feature of traditional music. These days most traditional players are able to read music fluently, but ear learning is still the preferred method for acquiring new tunes. When traditional musicians get together and swap tunes, they usually do so by listening to one another, playing and repeating phrases until they've got the melody.

This process can seem daunting to classical musicians used to learning from notation. It really isn't; although the traditional player doesn't have the music in front of them, they are running through a mental check-list whenever picking up a new tune, and there is certainly nothing 'mystical' about acquiring a tune by ear. Firstly, if you know the tune type (jig, reel, etc.), you also know the time signature and underlying feel of the tune. Next, work out the tune structure: how many parts are there? Are they the same length? Are they repeated? Once you've got these basics, focus on a few bars of the A part and try to copy them; to begin with, this might take several hearings. When you've got the first bars, move on to the next couple, working gradually through the whole tune. In this way, the tune is broken down into manageable chunks, and there's no separate process between getting the notes and memorizing them; it's a very efficient way of learning. Like all things, it takes practice; the more you do it, the easier it will become, and you'll be surprised at how quickly you'll go from being able to learn just a few bars at a time to learning half an A part within a couple of hearings.

Listening to traditional music this closely also teaches a huge amount about the feel of the music, where the stresses fall, which ornaments tend to be used in particular places, and how to vary passages of the tune. The 'Next steps' section at the end of each workshop gently encourages this process by asking you to listen to the second time through the tune, to play 'spot the difference', and to try to work out how to play what's changed. Developing these listening skills is absolutely key to getting under the skin of traditional music and to acquiring all the subtleties of bowing and ornamentation that give each style its own, distinct feel.

Some final thoughts

The fact that no fewer than eight regional fiddle styles are introduced in this book reflects the rich diversity of traditional music within England, Ireland, Scotland, and Wales. There are, of course, many other styles to be found in these lands, but this book offers a broadly representative range and, importantly, includes ideas from leading ambassadors for these regions.

Almost without exception, the regional styles explored in this volume have endured changing fortunes over time, with the twin themes of revival and regeneration predominating during the twentieth century. When writing their chapters, several contributors gave examples that reflect this journey and a strong sense of commitment, among individuals and communities, to adapt and embrace change. Particular fiddlers, tune collectors, and organizations were crucial in keeping distinctive, regional playing styles alive, no more so than in Ireland:

> By the 1980s the loss of distinctive regional sounds and repertoires was keenly felt ... Cairdeas na bhFidiléirí was established to preserve and promote the Donegal style [and has] played a central role in documenting the older tradition and in regenerating it through a teaching programme which has yielded a whole new generation of fiddle players. (*Liz Doherty*)

This sense of evolving traditions has also shaped the music of southern England, for example. We've seen the resurgence of a distinctive style from the 1990s onwards, driven by players such as Chris Wood and John Dipper of the English Acoustic Collective, and a conscious desire to reinterpret old tunes. For some, the approach to music-making and personal intent are also crucial:

> We have inherited a tradition that we know was once rich, complex, and beautiful, but has taken its fair share of knocks in the last few hundred years. For me, the joy of 'English fiddle music' is that *music* is the most important word in that phrase; if the music I make sounds how I want it to, then that alone justifies reinvigorating the tradition by using a borrowed technique or feature. After all, how does any tradition survive without adapting and assimilating other influences? I subscribe to the notion that tradition is not the worship of ashes, but the preservation of fire! (*John Dipper*)

The eight contributors to this book are very much individual musicians, offering their own, unique angle; they have all acknowledged that there are many ways to bring out the playing qualities associated with their region:

> A critical part of the process of learning to play Irish traditional music is developing your own voice; ultimately what you are trying to achieve is a set of skills and techniques which, over time, will be incorporated in a way that is personal to you, yet acceptable within the framework of the tradition. (*Liz Doherty*)

> When playing this music, take the time to learn the tune well enough for you to relax into it and to let the music play you. Only once this crucial step has been reached can you make the tune yours, let it tell your story, describe your locality and landscape, and allow the music to communicate your passion. (*John Dipper*)

1

NANCY KERR

Northumbrian 3/2 hornpipes

> Our Northumbrian pipe music being generally composed for social amusement, is written most frequently in triple and compound triple time … The performer, ever and anon reverting to the Air, indulges in variations prompted by his own genius.
>
> *Mr J. C. Fenwick, to the Society of Antiquaries of Newcastle, 1857*

Background

The north-east English county of Northumberland has a rich living tradition of music and song. Social dance is central to the tune repertoire, with rants, hornpipes, and slip jigs particularly popular with dance bands. The tradition is also firmly shaped by the popularity of the Northumbrian small-pipes, with their own repertoire of intricate and distinctive melodies.

As a young fiddle player in Northumberland, I was lucky to hear the great 'shepherd' musicians: fiddler Will Taylor, piper Joe Hutton, and Will Atkinson on harmonica (or 'moothie'). Superb players such as Emma Reid and Kathryn Tickell also draw inspiration from the style and repertoire of the region.

Style and tunes

The tunes in this chapter are 3/2 hornpipes, which are growing in popularity among fiddlers—3/2 is an energetic and catchy time signature to bow. Historically, 3/2 hornpipes have been more closely associated with the Northumbrian pipes, and learning tunes from another instrument can provide challenges when finding ways to 'swing' them on the fiddle. Using separate bows and occasional slurs in particular combinations works well, capturing on the fiddle the precise yet smooth textures a fine piper can achieve.

Of the tunes in this chapter, 'Rusty Gulley' is very popular among fiddlers. 'Lang Stayed Away' can be found, with several other 3/2 hornpipes, in Bruce and Stokoe's *Northumbrian Minstrelsy*—a great collection of songs and small-pipe tunes published in 1882. 'Bob and Joan' is a tune I learned from my parents, and I love its minor key and the amount of space in its melody.

Tap: track 1; Performance: track 2

Rusty Gulley

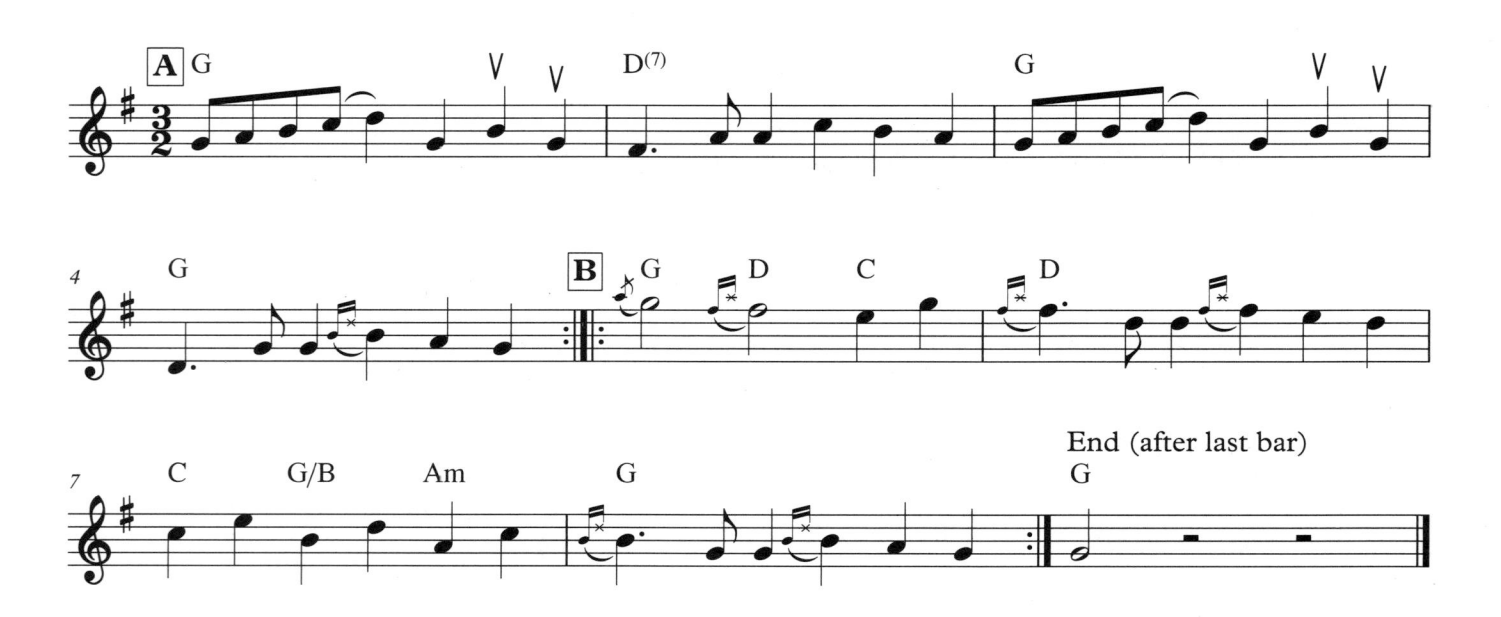

Slurred up-bows
In bars 1 and 3, try slurring the C and D together, as shown, in the middle of the bow. Occasional slurs, in the right places, can add smoothness and subtle syncopation—an effect fiddlers often call 'swing'—to the tune without losing the rhythmic energy that separate bows give you.

Double up-bows
Finish bars 1 and 3 with two consecutive Vs for a rhythmic, 'choppy' effect. Use plenty of bow for the Vs and don't play them too staccato—keep your right hand relaxed to preserve the flow of the notes.

Tap
In bar 4, ornament the B by 'tapping' the string with your third finger (see also 'Cut', pp. 25 and 41, and Double grace-note, p. 19). Don't touch the fingerboard—it should be more of a percussive tap than a note. *Listen to track 1 and then try playing it.*

Also play taps on the Bs in bar 8 and the F♯s in bars 5 and 6.

Cut from above
At the start of the B part, ornament the top G by playing a very short, clean grace-note A just before the beat. I call this a 'cut from above', and its sound reminds me of the Northumbrian pipes.

Next steps
Listen to how I add double-stops to the A part on the second time through the tune by playing the open G string beneath the melody; this adds rhythmic interest. Can you work out where to play the open Gs?

The Rusty Gulley

Performance: track 3

Lang Stayed Away

Performance: track 4

Bob and Joan

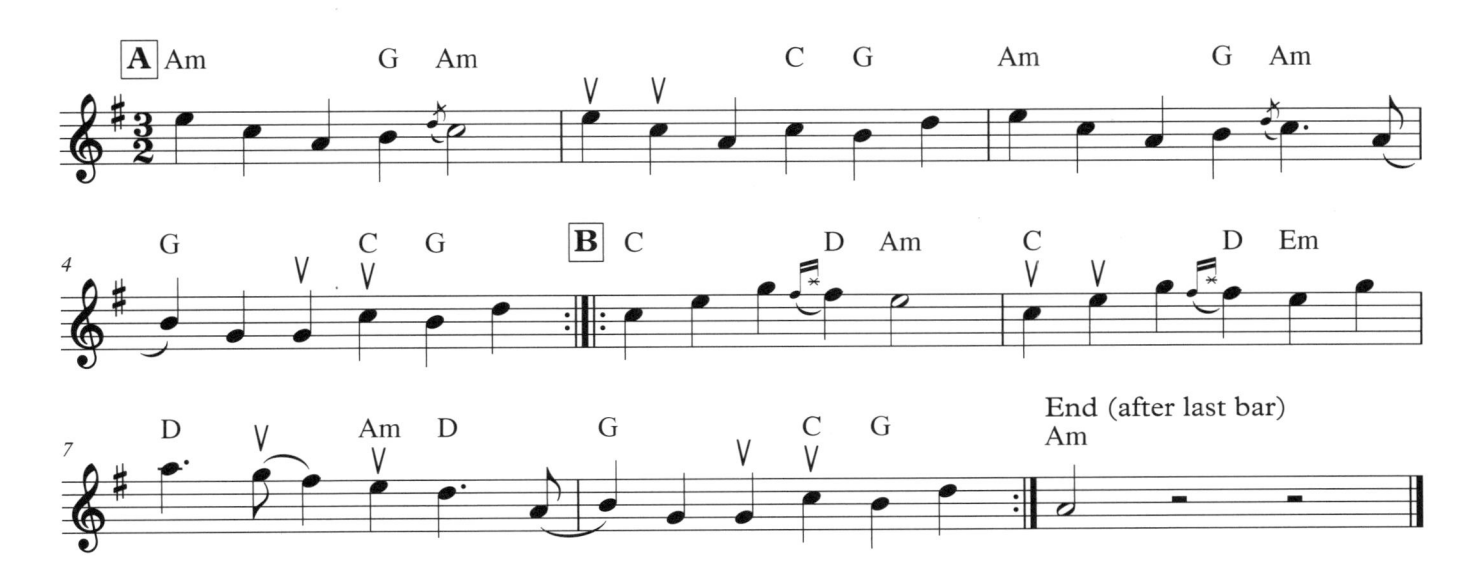

2
JENNA REID
Shetland reels

Unless you can play the fiddle wi' a lilt in til it, then that was no use even grapping a bow—it's the bowing and the lilt that makes you feel like dancing.

John Murdoch Henderson, Shetland fiddler (1902–72)

Background

The fiddle music of Shetland can be traced back to the 1700s. The *Statistical Account of Scotland* from 1794 states that 'music and dancing are favourite amusements especially in winter. Many of the common people play with skill upon the violin'. In Shetland, music was once woven into everyday life, as reflected in the Greenland whaling tunes, wedding music, and fiddle tunes named after fishing and trades. Fiddle music went hand-in-hand with dancing; as a result, the repertoire is dominated by reels that work well with the intricate steps found in traditional Shetland dances. The Shetland fiddle tradition is also strongly influenced by Shetland's historical links to Norway.

Prominent Shetland fiddlers include: Dr Tom Anderson (1910–91), who collected and published tunes from all over Shetland, was a founder member of the Shetland Fiddlers' Society, and worked tirelessly to bring about fiddle tuition in schools; Willie Hunter (1933–94), one of Shetland's most celebrated fiddlers and dedicated teachers; and Aly Bain (b. 1946), who enjoys an international performing, recording, and television career.

Style and tunes

In Shetland reels, the bowing is unique, with distinctive features including the 'driving' slurred up-bow that gives the tune lift and emphasizes the off-beats. Another characteristic is the use of 'ringing strings' double-stops, which displays a direct link to the Norwegian hardanger fiddle and its sympathetic drone strings.

'Aa the Ships ir Sailin'' I learned at a young age, probably with the Shetland Fiddlers' Society. 'Shelder Geö' is a place in the north of Shetland where oystercatchers ('shelders') nest, and this tune describes the sound they make. 'Mak a Kishie Needle, Dye' means 'make a kishie needle, grandad'. A kishie is a round basket, made with a wooden needle, that was used to carry peats home.

Performance: track 5

Aa the Ships ir Sailin'

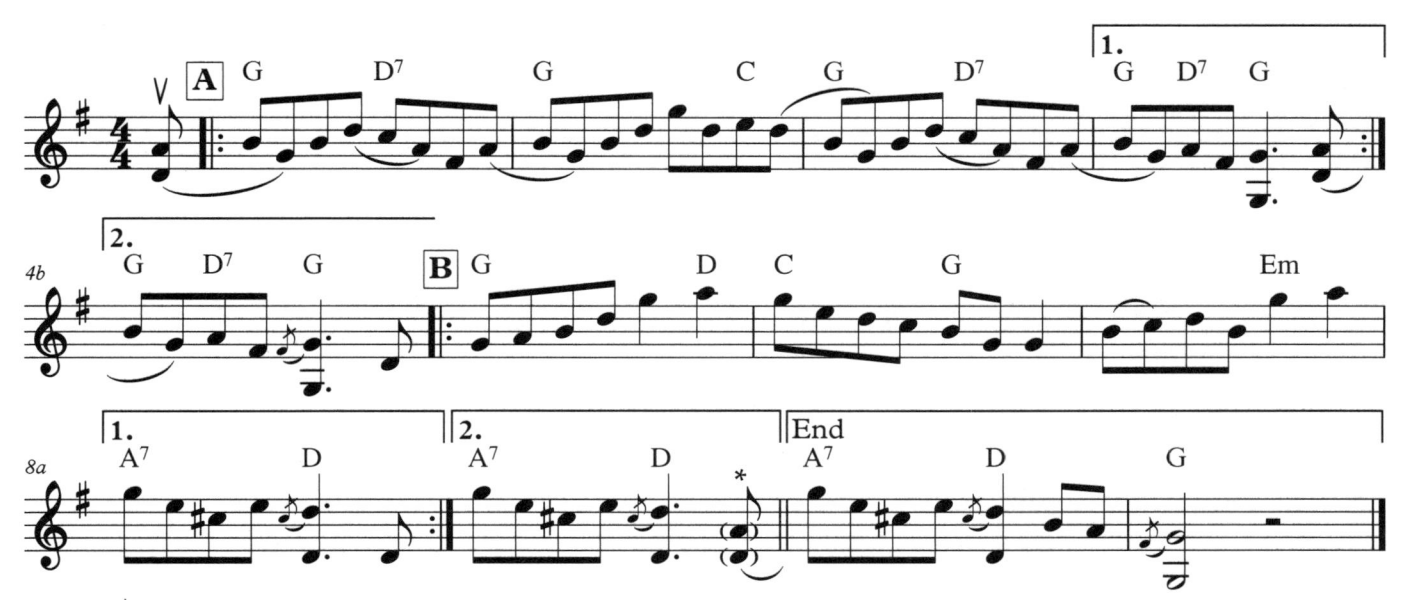

* Omit ♪ when going into 'Shelder Geö'.

Slurred up-bows

Slur the first three notes in an V, as shown. This bowing pattern is common in Shetland reels and gives a distinctive 'driving' V sound. Bowing over the barline also gives the tune a sense of lift and syncopation by emphasizing the off-beats (beats 2 and 4) with a strong ⊓.

This slurring pattern occurs throughout the whole A part of this reel. I would suggest playing the A part with shorter bows between the middle and the point.

The pattern varies slightly in bar 7, where the first two notes are slurred together, again on an V. Use longer bows for the ♩s in the B part.

'Ringing strings' double-stops

Notice the open D double-stop given beneath the first note. It was often a solo fiddler who would play for dancing in Shetland, and so double-stops—'ringing strings'—were used to increase the fiddler's volume so that the music could be heard above the dancers' feet.

Try adding the open G to the ♩. in bars 4*a* and *b*, using a long ⊓; make sure you get to the heel of the bow on the ♪ before. Do the same with the open D in bars 8*a*, *b*, and *c*.

Grace-note

Add a grace-note to bar 4*b*, as shown. Play it quickly, before the down-beat, but with the open G.

Using grace-notes in this way is very common in Shetland fiddling. Playing the grace-note with the octave ringing strings creates a discord, giving the tune real character. Note the similar grace-notes in bars 8*a*, *b*, and *c*.

Next steps

Varying the bowing when repeating a tune immediately changes the feel and stops things from being too repetitive. In the second playing of the A part, I use mainly separate bows, with just a few slurs. Can you copy this?

Performance: track 6

Shelder Geö

*Slur applies to first playing of the tune and A-part repeat. If repeating the tune, omit the pick-up (anacrusis) and slur the ♪♪ on an V.

Performance: track 7

Mak a Kishie Needle, Dye

*Slur applies to A-part repeat only.

3

JOHN DIPPER
Southern English Playford and morris dance tunes

Background

Very little is known about English fiddle music before the Industrial Revolution, but England's proximity to countries with complex fiddling traditions, the study of barrel organ rolls, and the evidence in the John Clare and Joseph Barnes manuscripts suggest that English fiddling may have shared many of the traits associated with Irish, Scottish, and American styles of the time. However, during much of the twentieth century, English fiddle music was often regarded as simple and plain. We are left to surmise that during the Industrial Revolution and much of the Victorian era, the fiddle and its repertoire became largely forgotten, superseded by new fashions, among them brass bands and imported tunes such as the polka and waltz. It also seems likely that the fiddle lost out to the advance of new technology in the form of louder, cheaper polyphonic squeezeboxes.

Chris Wood and pioneering ensemble the English Acoustic Collective are among a number of key players who have contributed significantly in recent years to the resurgence and redefining of southern English fiddle music. Other notable fiddlers are Chris Bartram, Paul Burgess, Mat Green, Tom Moore, Miranda Rutter, Dave Shepherd, and Sam Sweeney.

Style and tunes

It is essential to remember that most English repertoire is music for dancing. The techniques introduced in this workshop are designed to help you perform these tunes with drive, groove, and subtlety, so that they can be performed equally in a session or in a concert setting, all the while being irresistible to the dancer!

'Argiers' can be found on the first page of the first edition of John Playford's *English Dancing Master*, dated 1651. 'Old Tom of Oxford' is a morris dance tune from Oxfordshire, and 'Mount Hills' is also from Playford. Both Playford tunes have specific dances that are notated in the original manuscript, but the tunes are now more usually performed in a concert setting.

Pulsed bowing: track 8; Bowed treble: track 9; Trill: track 10; Performance: track 11

Argiers

Pulsed bowing

Emphasizing the off-beats instantly breathes life into the tune, and using the pulsed bow technique is one of the most effective ways to do this.

Listen to track 8 and then try the exercise below. The dashed slurs indicate pulsed bowing. Use approximately a third of the bow for the first ♩ in each pair, then increase the weight and speed of the bow to accent the second ♩, using the rest of the bow.

Practise this technique by accompanying the melody on track 11, using the open A throughout.

This pulse template underpins your approach to the melody; the off-beat emphasis enhances the melody in certain bars. The places that really leap out for me are the long notes at the end of each half of the tune, as indicated.

8

Rhythmic variation

Let's add rhythm and groove to the A part by emphasizing the fourth and eighth ♪s in bar 1 by combining slurs and rests, as shown. Try this also in bars 3 and 4.

In the original Playford manuscript, there is a ♩ on beat 2 of bar 4. It has been changed here into ♩. ♪ to emphasize the last ♪ in the bar.

Bowed treble

Add a bowed treble to the last ♩ of bars 6 and 14, as indicated, starting on an V. I play trebles in the middle of the bow and tighten my forearm muscles briefly so that the wrist and hand 'shivers' (see also 'Bowed treble', p. 13, and 'Birl', p. 25). The treble adds a superb emphasis to the note. *Listen to track 9 to hear how to play it.*

Slurred triplet

Use a slurred triplet run on the final ♩ in bar 11, as indicated, to build up to the peak note of the phrase.

Trill

Add short trills (mordents) as indicated by ∿. *Listen carefully to track 10; they should be played like this:*

Double-stops

In the B part, there are many opportunities to use double-stopping to accent or to change the feel. In bars 9–13, do this by mixing on- and off-beat accents, as notated.

Next steps

In the repeat of the A part during the second playing, I vary the melody by changing the pitch of beat 2 in bar 3 and the last note in bar 4. Can you identify and play the substitute notes?

Performance: track 12

Old Tom of Oxford

Performance: track 13

Mount Hills

4

LIZ DOHERTY
Donegal reels

Background

County Donegal, in the north-west of Ireland, is known for its distinctive style of traditional fiddle music. The style, and its associated repertoire, displays many unique features that distinguish it from other prominent Irish styles, and it also boasts many influences from the Scottish tradition.

In Ireland, throughout much of the twentieth century, a noticeable shift took place from local and regional styles towards a more uniform sound, thanks to the advent of recordings, radio, publications, and various changes to the context of music-making, including the separation of music and dance. In Donegal, a concerted effort was made to capture the unique elements of the local traditions and an organization, Cairdeas na bhFidiléirí, was established in the 1980s. This is dedicated to the preservation and promotion of the Donegal style, particularly as it is practised in the south-west of the county.

The Donegal style now enjoys a high profile within the wider Irish music community. Altan, one of the tradition's most commercially successful bands, has brought the local music onto an international platform, as have artists such as Tommy Peoples and Fidil. Other notable fiddlers, past and present, include John Byrne, Vincent Campbell, John Doherty, and Seamus Grant.

Style and tunes

Reels constitute the largest part of the Donegal repertoire, as elsewhere in Ireland. The style is often regarded as being quite aggressive, a reference to the preferred bowing, which consists mainly of single strokes. The emphasis is on placing the strong bow—the down-bow—on the down-beats of each bar (beats 1 and 3). However, slurs do occur, and they play an important role in organizing the bow direction so that down-bows fall on down-beats.

'Leslie's Reel' is a popular tune associated with the Leslie brothers from Glencolmcille in Donegal. 'Dinkie Dorrian's' was almost certainly composed by Francie 'Dearg' O'Beirne and became a favourite of step-dancer Con 'Dinkie' Dorrian. The title has become corrupted and the tune is sometimes known as 'The Dinky Dory', which shows the oral tradition at its best! 'The Boys of Malin' is a popular session reel.

Bowed treble: track 14; Bowed triplet: track 15; Single grace-note: track 16; Performance: track 17

Leslie's Reel

* If going into 'Dinkie Dorrian's', replace the F♯ with a D.

Down-bow up-slur bowing

The whole tune uses a ♩ ♫ pattern. Start the tune in the upper-half, but not at the tip. Notice that all the strong beats are played on a ⊓. Accentuate them by giving the bow an extra-long pull, also applying extra weight.

Bowed treble

The treble is a popular ornament in the Donegal style (see also 'Bowed treble', p. 9, and 'Birl', p. 25). It adds an agitated rhythmic interest and is used where a ♩ is found in the tune. It sounds like ♫♪, as indicated. The key to executing trebles successfully is bow control. Very little arm movement is required; a mere flick of the wrist is sufficient, and I find that I tighten my forearm to manage this.

Listen to track 14, then try the treble in bar 1 slowly. Start in the middle of the bow and apply plenty of pressure—lean hard on the strings. Bow ⊓ V ⊓ and dig right into the first note, easing the pressure slightly over notes 2 and 3.

You should aim to create quite a rough, 'squawking' sound when playing the treble slowly; the more grating it is, the better it will sound at speed.

Practise the bowed treble followed by the ♫ in bar 1 in isolation, and then as indicated elsewhere.

Bowed triplet

The bowed triplet is played like the treble but with three consecutive pitches rather than on the same note. Where a ⊓ is required for a following down-beat, slur out of the triplet. Try this in bars 4–5.

Single grace-note

Add grace-notes to bars 2 and 6, as indicated, to separate two notes of the same pitch. The single grace-note is used especially, though not exclusively, for this purpose, and it is generally played with the third finger. It accents, and is crushed almost on top of, the following melody note, and is played in the same bow. The pitch of the grace-note should barely be heard; the finger merely flicks the string, and the effect should be of a short, rhythmic bite.

In bars 12 and 15, the grace-notes are played in the same way, although here they don't separate notes of the same pitch.

Double-stops

A typical feature of the Donegal style is the frequent use of double-stops. Try adding the open A under the melody note in bars 9 and 14, as shown.

Next steps

On the second playing of the A part, I add character to some first-finger F♯s by putting my finger down on the E string a little lower than the required pitch and sliding quickly and lightly up to the correct note. Can you copy how this sounds, and then add it to the F♯s in these places?

Performance: track 18

Dinkie Dorrian's

*Omit pick-up (anacrusis) if preceded by 'Leslie's Reel'.
† Optional doubling.

Link for 'The Boys of Malin' (replaces last bar)

End (replaces last bar)

Performance: track 19

The Boys of Malin

* Optional doubling.

5
LIZ DOHERTY
Donegal jigs

Background (as Donegal reels)

County Donegal, in the north-west of Ireland, is known for its distinctive style of traditional fiddle music. The style, and its associated repertoire, displays many unique features that distinguish it from other prominent Irish styles, and it also boasts many influences from the Scottish tradition.

In Ireland, throughout much of the twentieth century, a noticeable shift took place from local and regional styles towards a more uniform sound, thanks to the advent of recordings, radio, publications, and various changes to the context of music-making, including the separation of music and dance. In Donegal, a concerted effort was made to capture the unique elements of the local traditions and an organization, Cairdeas na bhFidiléirí, was established in the 1980s. This is dedicated to the preservation and promotion of the Donegal style, particularly as it is practised in the south-west of the country.

The Donegal style now enjoys a high profile within the wider Irish music community. Altan, one of the tradition's most commercially successful bands, has brought the local music onto an international platform, as have artists such as Tommy Peoples and Fidil. Other notable fiddlers, past and present, include John Byrne, Vincent Campbell, John Doherty, and Seamus Grant.

Style and tunes

Jigs are one of the most popular of the dance tune forms. Four variants exist: the double jig, single jig, slide, and slip jig. Of these, the double jig in 6/8 time is the most common and is the variant referred to simply as 'the jig'. In jig playing, the particular 'lilt' or 'swing' associated with the Irish style is achieved by stretching the first ♪ in each group of three, falling slightly short of making it a dotted note. There should also be a strong emphasis on the first note of beat 1 and a lesser emphasis on the first note of beat 2, and this requires care with the bowing; as in Donegal reels, the strong first beats are played with ⊓s, with V slurs (typically at the end of bars) being used to organize this pattern.

'Johnny Boyle's Jig' has an unusual structure, with repeated A and B parts but a single C part. The second tune is associated with Donegal fiddler Con Cassidy (1909–94), who was known for his distinctive repertoire and style. 'The Black Rogue' is a popular session tune played throughout Ireland.

Double grace-note: track 20; Performance: track 21

Johnny Boyle's Jig

* Also use the End bar when going into 'Con Cassidy's Jig'; shorten the ♩. to a ♩ and play the pick-up (anacrusis) given in the next tune.

Combining down-bow strong beats and up-bow slurs

The usual pattern is to play a ⊓ on beat 1 and to end the bar on an V, slurring where necessary to achieve this, e.g. bars 1, 3, and 5. Note that the first ♪ in each group of three is stretched slightly to create lilt; *listen carefully to this effect on the CD.*

Double up-bows

At the end of a phrase or section where the last-beat rhythm is ♩ ♪ (as at bar 8*b*), use V V to separate the notes. Stop the bow but keep it on the string. Slightly lengthen the ♩ and then accent the following ♪

Double semiquavers (bowed treble/triplet)

Add rhythmic interest to ♪♪♪ groups by substituting the first ♪ with two ♬s to create bowed trebles/triplets as explained on p. 13. The ♬s are always bowed ⊓ V, but the following notes may be slurred or separate depending on their position in the bar. Try this in bars 4 and 20.

Single grace-note

Add single grace-notes, as explained on p. 13, where indicated.

Double grace-note

The double grace-note (bar 19) is typically used when the melody line is descending by step in ♪s. *Listen carefully to track 20 to hear how it is played.* The upper grace-note is played with a flicked finger and, as with the single grace-note, the third finger is generally used. (See 'Tap', p. 2, and 'Cut', pp. 25 and 41.)

Double-stops

Add double-stops as marked. In addition, try playing the open D string with any third-finger D to create an intermittent drone.

Octave transposition

Try playing the B part an octave lower than written, returning to pitch on the last note of bar 16*b*. This is particularly effective when two or more melody instruments are playing the tune. Playing an octave apart is common in a number of fiddle traditions and dates back to when added volume was needed pre-amplification.

Next steps

On the second playing of the B part, I play an octave lower than notated. Listen to how I change the rhythm and feel of bar 11 by adding a passing note B between the two As on the first beat. Can you add this variation? I make the same change in bar 15.

Performance: track 22

Con Cassidy's Jig

*Omit ♪ when going into 'The Black Rogue'.

Performance: track 23

The Black Rogue

*If playing the B part an octave lower, return to the notated pitch at bar 15.

6

AIDAN O'ROURKE
West Highland strathspeys and a reel

Background

Bagpipe and clàrsach (harp) music in the West Highlands of Scotland pre-date the introduction of the fiddle, but there are accounts from over three hundred years ago that prove fiddling was popular throughout the region. Records from 1703 reveal that on the Isle of Lewis there were '18 men who play on the violin pretty well without being taught', while Estate records from Dunvegan on the Isle of Skye show payments in 1706 to 'violer' James Glass.

After the Jacobite rebellion of 1745, bagpipes were banned, and in many ways the fiddle temporarily replaced the bagpipes as Scotland's national instrument. The fiddle remained popular until Calvinism swept the West Highlands at the end of the eighteenth century. The church disapproved of dancing and fiddle playing and there are reports of the burning of fiddles on the Isle of Skye in 1805.

There was a great resurgence of West Highland fiddle playing during the twentieth century and current fiddlers of note include Angus Grant (*senior* and *junior*), Allan and Ewen Henderson, Iain MacFarlane, Archie McAllister, Eilidh Shaw, and Alasdair White.

Style and tunes

The West Highland style is characterized by lilting, lyrical phrases that have their origins in the Gaelic language. The style is also influenced by bagpipe music and ornamentation, and a West Highland fiddler's repertoire will include many pipe tunes. Common tune types include strathspeys, which are played more fluidly in the West Highland style than in the more angular East Coast fashion, and reels, which have an emphasized down-beat and tend to be less swung than in Shetland or many parts of Ireland.

There are two strathspeys and one reel in this chapter; these two kinds of tune are often played together in sets, and the features discussed here apply to both types of tune. 'Mrs MacLeod's Strathspey' appears in *The Athole Collection of the Dance Music of Scotland* as a reel called 'Bonnie Annie'. It was composed by Daniel Dow and has been popular in Scotland since the eighteenth century. There's much confusion as to the origins of 'Niel Gow's Wife'; it first appears as 'Mr MacDonald of Staffa's Strathspey' in 1794, but the fiddler Niel Gow (1727–1807) and his sons published it with the title given here in 1802, crediting Niel Gow as composer. 'Lochiel's Awa' Tae France' is a great old Highland reel. The full title is 'Lochiel's Awa' Tae France But He'll Come Back Again'; it refers to John Cameron of Lochiel, who fought in the Battle of Glen Shiel in 1719. In defeat, he fled to France, and never returned to Scotland.

Birl: track 24; Cut: track 25; Performance: track 26

Mrs MacLeod's Strathspey

Daniel Dow

* Omit the last beat of bar 12a when going into 'Niel Gow's Wife'.

Strathspey rhythm

The strathspey dotted rhythm is very distinctive and incorporates the ♪♩ pattern known as the 'Scotch snap'. *Listen to track 26 to hear how the rhythms are played*; it is characteristic to lengthen the dotted notes, and to shorten and accent the ♪s.

Practise this by repeating bar 3 (without the ornament), starting on a ⊓ near the point. Articulate the notes with care; use plenty of bow on the dotted notes so that the ♪s are played in the top half of the bow.

Birl

The birl is one of the most common features in West Highland fiddling (see also 'Bowed treble', pp. 9 and 13). It is played near the tip of the bow (I use the top 20cm), so take care to keep in the upper-half on approach. It is usually bowed ⊓ V ⊓, and I articulate it with a flick of the wrist rather than with the arm. Apply pressure on the bow on the first ⊓ to make it crisp and clear.

Try the birl on the first beat of bar 1. Often written as a ♪♪♩ (as here), the birl's actual rhythm sounds more like ♪♪♩ (as indicated above the stave), with the first two notes played very quickly. *Listen to this on track 24*.

Combining separate and slurred bows

The tune starts on an V so that you have a strong ⊓ to start the birl; slur together the two notes after the birl (see also 'down-bow up-slur bowing', p. 13). This is a common bowing pattern that recurs in the A part. The slurs in bars 5 and 10 provide variety.

Cut

Add a cut, as indicated by ♪, to bar 1, and as marked elsewhere. This is a key ornament I use and it can be applied frequently to all types of tunes. I use the third finger where possible. The finger flicks the string to 'cut' the note; take care it touches only the string, and not the fingerboard. *Listen to track 25 to hear how to play it*. (See also 'Tap', p. 2, 'Double grace-note', p. 19, and 'Cut', p. 41.)

Grace-note

Add a grace-note to beat 3 of bar 2, as marked. It is slurred into beat 3 slightly ahead of the beat. Use similar grace-notes where indicated.

Next steps

On the second playing of the tune, I add an emphasis to the last beat of bar 10 by playing an open G below the notated pitch; adding double-stops in such places enhances the rhythmic feel. Have a go at playing it.

Performance: track 27

Niel Gow's Wife

* Slur does not apply if preceded by 'Mrs MacLeod's Strathspey'.
† If going into 'Lochiel's Awa' Tae France', rall. on the last three notes of this tune.

Performance: track 28

Lochiel's Awa' Tae France

*Omit the pick-up (anacrusis) if coming out of 'Niel Gow's Wife' and pick up the tempo in the first bar.

7

SIÂN PHILLIPS
Welsh hornpipes

Background

It seems that the violin was first introduced into Welsh folk music around 1700 by the Welsh Romany Abram Wood. It rapidly superseded its predecessors the crwth and the rascal (both types of bowed lyre, also referred to as fiddles), and became established, alongside the harp, as one of the most popular instruments in Wales. However, the fiddle tradition appears to have fared badly during the religious revivals of the nineteenth century, existing only in isolated pockets by the early twentieth century.

Alongside a more general promotion of the Welsh language and folk tunes from the 1960s onwards, the fiddle reclaimed its role in Welsh music. Among my own influences while growing up was the fiddler Graham Pritchard, who played with the ground-breaking folk bands Mynediad Am Ddim and Ar Log during the 1970s and 1980s. The significance of Welsh fiddling was recognized in 1997 with the recording *Ffidil*, which brought many Welsh fiddlers and their music into view, among them Bernard and Gerard Kilbride, Mike Lease, Stephen Rees, Jane Ridout, and Huw Roberts.

Style and tunes

Welsh fiddle style owes much to Baroque bowing techniques and English dance influences. The repertoire is drawn from three distinct strands: gypsy, dance, and 'mouth' music, the latter being the singing of tunes to scat syllables (also known as 'diddling'). Marches, jigs, slip jigs, waltzes, and hornpipes all feature, but few reels; those that do are played as hornpipes, like the 'Gower Reel' in this chapter. Hornpipes have a distinctive dotted rhythm (although they are often notated in straight quavers) and 2/2 feel, brought to life by 'swing' bowing.

'Gower Reel' is transcribed from a recording of Phil Tanner's diddling, and 'Swansea Hornpipe' is credited to the harpist Nansi Richards, whose playing was influenced by the gypsies who stayed on her farm. 'Pibddawns y Car Gwyllt' ('The Wild Car Hornpipe') was passed to me by Dan Morris, a fiddler from Dolgellau in north Wales. The title refers to the unique method Graig Ddu quarry workers had for getting home quickly at the end of the day, on crude, rail-mounted trolleys, or 'wild cars'.

Swing bowing: track 29; Performance: track 30

Gower Reel

*The C does not need to be accurately pitched.

Slurring across the beat

'Swing' bowing—slurring across the beat—is particularly effective in bringing out the 'lolloping' hornpipe rhythm (see also 'Slurred up-bows', p. 2). *Listen to the basic pattern below on track 29, then try playing it, using plenty of bow and putting a light emphasis or 'lean' on the ♪s:*

Two swing-bowing patterns appear in this tune. The first is the '3–3–2' pattern, so-called because it creates three groups of notes in the bar; see bars 1, 5, and 13. The slur falls across the second and third beats. Simpler versions of this pattern, maintaining the slur across the second and third beats, appear in bars 2, 6, and 14.

The second pattern is one ⊓ followed by three notes slurred together on an V. This pattern occurs in bar 10. Play the ⊓ with an unaccented fast bow-stroke to allow for plenty of bow on the subsequent three notes.

Sometimes the slurring pattern changes to vary the feel created by the swing bowing, e.g. bars 3 and 4, where ♩.♪ pairs are slurred together.

Slurring out of the bar

Slurring the last note of the bar into the first note of the following bar helps to create a sense of 'lilt'. Try this in bars 3–4.

Double up-bows

Play V V, coming out of the slur, in bars 6 and 14. The V V should be lightly detached and can come off the string; keep the wrist relaxed and aim for a 'cheeky' effect. Also try this in bar 11.

Triplets

These are used to add interest in place of straight ♩s and to add 'passing notes' between pairs of ♪s, and can be played separately or slurred. Here, the ♩♩♩s are all played separately, starting on either bow direction.

Unlike in other styles, the ♩♩♩s serve a melodic rather than percussive function, with the rhythm exactly as written.

Left-hand ornamentation

Because of the extensive use of melodic ♩♩♩s, I would tend not to include any left-hand decoration in this tune.

Next steps

I sometimes add an ascending ♩♩♩ run during the crotchet rests to keep a sense of momentum. Here, I do this going into the second time through the tune, and also at the end of the A part. Can you work out the notes and add the ♩♩♩s?

Performance: track 31

Swansea Hornpipe

* Omit rest if going into 'Pibddawns y Car Gwyllt'.

Performance: track 32

Pibddawns y Car Gwyllt

8

PATSY REID
North-East Scottish slow airs

Background

Scotland has a rich and varied fiddle tradition that pre-dates the arrival of the modern violin in the British Isles around 1660. Before then, more primitive bowed instruments such as the viol, rebec, and crwth were popular, but within a decade the fiddle had become, alongside the bagpipes, one of Scotland's national instruments.

The North-East Scottish fiddle style broadly encompasses the playing traditions found in Moray, Aberdeenshire, Angus, and Highland Perthshire, and it is essentially a notated rather than aural tradition. It is well preserved because of its written form and its place in the strong competition circuit in Scotland. Celebrated composers include Niel Gow (1727–1807), William Marshall (1748–1833), Peter Milne (1824–1908), and James Scott Skinner (1843–1927). Unsurprisingly, given the time in which several of these fiddler–composers were writing, they absorbed many traits from classical music of the Romantic period, and this is reflected in the North-East style. Current notable players include Paul Anderson and Douglas Lawrence.

Style and tunes

The North-East style is elegant, flamboyant, and robust, and slow airs make use of what are usually thought of as predominantly classical skills such as vibrato, a broad range of tone, position shifts, advanced bow distribution, and rubato. In addition, a stylish slow air performance requires a good sense of phrasing, excellent intonation, and the use of left-hand ornamentation.

I performed all of the tunes in this chapter when I was competing in fiddle competitions around Scotland. 'The Marchioness of Huntly's Favourite' is by William Marshall and was dedicated to Elizabeth Brodie, a pianist and the wife of the Marquis of Huntly. The couple were firm supporters of Marshall's music and instrumental in the publication of his 1822 collection of tunes. 'Bovaglie's Plaid' is by James Scott Skinner and refers to the local saying that the wood around Bovaglie Farm near Balmoral 'shelters Bovaglie ferm like a plaid'. Also by Skinner, 'The Weeping Birches of Kilmorack' was written after a train derailed near Beauly, mysteriously causing the nearby birch trees to wilt and die. These are all big, expressive tunes, so I would only play them once through. However, I have recorded two performances of each: the first as written, and with accompaniment; and the second as a slightly more developed version, played solo, as slow airs often are.

Performance 1 (as notated): track 33; Performance 2 (with variation): track 34

The Marchioness of Huntly's Favourite

William Marshall

Phrasing and rubato

Paying attention to the phrasing is essential for slow airs, and phrase marks have been included here to give a sense of how the tune should be played. There are natural 'breathing' points that must be observed if the tune is to sing. Broadly speaking, a phrase in a slow air should open smoothly, build in some way, conclude, and fade out.

Longer phrases often make use of rubato ('robbed' time), where the tempo is given flexibility according to the intensity of the phrase. The ninth phrase (bar 15) is the most dramatic part of the tune, so I rush into it slightly and then slow down again as the phrase ends. *Listen carefully to this effect on track 33.*

Organizing the bowing

Bow speed and distribution are crucial for creating the phrasing and tempo fluctuations discussed above. Take the bow's weight and natural dynamics into account; the sound decays on a long ⊓, which works well at the end of phrases. Here, the slurs allow most phrases to fade on a ⊓.

Listen to the silences that occur in the tune at the end of phrases 1, 2, 4, and 9; such moments of quiet add a great deal to slow air performance. Practise fading out entirely at these points, without lifting the bow off the string.

On occasion, it's necessary to create the fade-out effect on an V, e.g. mid-way through phrase 5 (end of bar 9). It takes lots of practice (and strong right-hand fingers!) to maintain a lovely, soft sound in such places.

I really take time on the last beat of bar 15. Employ a slower bow to achieve this effect.

Shifting and position work

In trickier keys such as this, it can be easier to move up to a higher position to avoid cumbersome string crossings, e.g. in bar 11.

Shifting also allows you to maintain a consistent tone and flow of the melody by staying on one string, e.g. in bar 9.

There are also opportunities in this tune for sliding (*portamento*) shifts, e.g. on the last beat of bars 7 and 11. Slide the finger you are already using up or down to the new position before playing the next note. It sounds great and is much easier than shifting silently!

Left-hand ornamentation

Grace-notes enhance the melody and instantly transform an 'ordinary' tune into a 'Scottish' tune! I use one-, two-, and three-note grace-notes here. It is impossible to notate the exact lengths; for example, the B♮ grace-note at the start of bars 1 and 3 is long (more like an appoggiatura), whereas the double grace-note at the start of bar 10 is much crisper and accents the first beat. *Listen carefully to track 33 to learn how to play them.*

Make sure that you have a solid sense of the melody before adding the grace-notes; they must not interfere with the underlying pulse.

Next steps

In the second performance of this tune, I play additional grace-notes. Listen especially to bars 10 and 14, where I ornament the second beat of each bar. Can you work out what the grace-notes are and then try adding them?

Performance 1 (as notated): track 35; Performance 2 (with variation): track 36

Bovaglie's Plaid

James Scott Skinner

Performance 1 (as notated): track 37; Performance 2 (with variation): track 38

The Weeping Birches of Kilmorack

James Scott Skinner

9
KEVIN BURKE
Sligo reels

Background
County Sligo is in the north-west of Ireland and is an area renowned for its music and musicians, particularly its fiddle and flute players. A blind fiddler called Tom Healy, born in the latter half of the nineteenth century, is credited as one of the earliest sources of today's Sligo style. In the 1920s recordings made in America by a handful of immigrant Sligo fiddlers became hugely influential all over Ireland; the three most prominent recorded players were Michael Coleman, James Morrison, and Paddy Killoran. The popularity of their recordings drew attention to Sligo's many great fiddlers, including Philip and 'Lad' O'Beirne, Michael Gorman, and 'Kippeen' Scanlon.

Style and tunes
Sligo playing is typically brisk and lively, with high energy for dancing. In northern parts of Ireland, tunes are usually played fast with short bow strokes; further south, typically in County Clare, they are played more slowly, with long, swooping bow strokes and sliding notes. Sligo, situated between both of these areas, has elements of both styles—the faster tempo of the north with the more ornamented fingering and longer bow strokes of Clare. This blend may well explain why the early recordings of Sligo players were so exhilarating to those hearing this music for the first time.

The Sligo repertoire consists of a wide variety of dance tunes—slip jigs, single jigs, hornpipes, waltzes, polkas, and more—but reels make up by far the largest group of tunes, followed closely by jigs.

Of the tunes in this chapter, 'Boys of the Lough' is a well-known reel, and it is one of Michael Coleman's most highly regarded recordings. 'Pigeon on the Gate' is a tune I learned as a child from a variety of sources. I initially learned 'Sligo Maid' from Paddy Killoran's recording, but I grew up hearing it played in so many different ways, and on different instruments, that my version is a composite. In addition to the features discussed in this workshop, 'Pigeon on the Gate' and 'Sligo Maid' also use bowed trebles (see pp. 9 and 13). My thanks to Betsy Branch, Portland, OR, for her assistance in transcribing the tunes.

Roll: track 39; Cut: track 40; Performance: track 41

Boys of the Lough

* Omit the last beat of bar 32 when going into 'Pigeon on the Gate'.

Slurring onto the beat

The underlying pattern is to slur 'onto' the down-beats, i.e. from beat 4 onto beat 1 and beat 2 onto beat 3. I think this practice of often ending slurs on the main beats and starting new bows on the off-beats is why the word 'lilt' is used in relation to Irish music.

This idea persists throughout the tune, as notated, but is not used all of the time. Occasionally, to add character, I vary the pattern, e.g. the second and third ♪s are slurred together in bar 10.

Slurred triplet

The skeleton version of the tune would have ♩s, suggesting scope for ornamentation, wherever the notation ♫♩ appears here. This ornament is referred to as a 'slurred triplet', but the Sligo fiddler would play the rhythm as notated. Try the simple version in bar 27, slurring on an V.

Play slurred triplets as indicated elsewhere; the slurring varies.

Roll

Rolls, indicated here by ∾, are also used to ornament ♩s. Look at the realized version of the roll in bar 13, as shown below. The F♯ is the ornamented note:

Think of the F♯ as being 'interrupted' by notes 2 and 4, which are not pitched clearly. The third finger merely taps the string on note 2 (without touching the fingerboard). The second finger does not lift fully to allow a proper E on note 4, but just enough to take the pressure off the string and interrupt the F♯. *Listen carefully to track 39 to hear how the roll sounds, then try it where indicated.*

Cut

Adding a cut between notes of the same pitch accents the beat. Try it where indicated by ♫—flick the finger onto the string without touching the fingerboard. *Listen to track 40 carefully; you will hear that the cut is played just after the beginning of the second note.* (See also 'Tap', p. 2, 'Double grace-note', p. 19, and 'Cut', p. 25.) The cut in bar 25 is placed mid-slur to keep the second beat well-defined without the need to change bow.

Grace-note

Try playing the grace-note as indicated just before the slurred triplet in bar 1. *Listen to track 41 to hear the lyrical effect this creates.* Use similar grace-notes as marked.

Triplet run

This device is widely used by Sligo players. In the skeleton tune, the melody line in bars 29 and 30 would descend in a run of ♪ couplets, each a third apart. As notated here, the couplets are converted into ♫♪s by adding the notes in-between each pair. Again, the ♫♪ is actually played as ♪♫, as notated.

Double-stops

Add double-stops, or drones, as notated. In each case, a melody note is held beneath or above subsequent melody notes on adjacent strings, e.g. bar 3, where the F♯ is sustained beneath the D and A ♪s on beats 3 and 4. In longer sequences, this approach to double-stopping creates a subtle but strong rhythmic effect typical of the style.

Next steps

Part of the art of playing Irish music is to add small changes into the melody to vary it each time it is played through. Listen to the way I play ♫♪s (♪♫s) on the first beats of bars 1 and 5 on the second playing; can you work out how to play these?

Performance: track 42

Pigeon on the Gate

* If coming out of 'Boys of the Lough', the pick-up (anacrusis) should be played as ♪
† Use dashed slur on repeat.
‡ Omit the last beat of bar 32 when going into 'Sligo Maid'.

End (replaces last bar)

Performance: track 43

Sligo Maid